YOUR KNOWLEDGE HAS VALUE

- We will publish your bachelor's and master's thesis, essays and papers

- Your own eBook and book - sold worldwide in all relevant shops

- Earn money with each sale

Upload your text at www.GRIN.com
and publish for free

Bibliographic information published by the German National Library:

The German National Library lists this publication in the National Bibliography; detailed bibliographic data are available on the Internet at http://dnb.dnb.de .

This book is copyright material and must not be copied, reproduced, transferred, distributed, leased, licensed or publicly performed or used in any way except as specifically permitted in writing by the publishers, as allowed under the terms and conditions under which it was purchased or as strictly permitted by applicable copyright law. Any unauthorized distribution or use of this text may be a direct infringement of the author s and publisher s rights and those responsible may be liable in law accordingly.

Imprint:

Copyright © 2017 GRIN Verlag, Open Publishing GmbH
Print and binding: Books on Demand GmbH, Norderstedt Germany
ISBN: 9783668427822

This book at GRIN:

http://www.grin.com/en/e-book/357879/about-service-and-creative-industry-theory

Anonym

About Service and Creative Industry Theory

GRIN Publishing

GRIN - Your knowledge has value

Since its foundation in 1998, GRIN has specialized in publishing academic texts by students, college teachers and other academics as e-book and printed book. The website www.grin.com is an ideal platform for presenting term papers, final papers, scientific essays, dissertations and specialist books.

Visit us on the internet:

http://www.grin.com/

http://www.facebook.com/grincom

http://www.twitter.com/grin_com

AN ESSAY ON SERVICE AND CREATIVE INDUSTRY THEORY

The economy of each and every nation and state across the globe is constituted of the major sectors which are an essential part of the growth. These include the primary sector- comprising of the extraction such as the mining and agriculture. The second sector is the secondary area which concentrates much on the manufacturing of the new products. The third and crucial area in the service industry or what is referred to as the tertiary sector. Most of the economies have the tendency to major and pay more of their attention to the manufacturing sector hoping for a revolution in the service or tertiary sector. However, in the recent past, the service industry has seen dramatic and unprecedented changes including cost reduction, speed, and improvements in reliability of transport and communication of the citizens.

This paper has substantially concentrated on the theory on service and the creative industry. The first part of the journal defines and shows the correlation between the services sector and the creative industry and also comes out with a definition that encompasses the both independent terms. The second part gives a brief but consequential history of how the service and creative industry has evolved throughout the history. The third part of this research paper shows the significance of the government and private sectors to engage in the service sector.

The fourth part of the research paper is dedicated to analyzing and explain the distinctive characteristics of the service and creative industry as compared to the other two sectors of the economy namely primary and secondary. The fifth and last part of the research paper entirely discusses the challenges that are facing the service and creative industry as well as the startup business being started by young people.

The service sector consists of the minor but crucial agents of the economy which include; tourism, education, social services, and banking. In the soft sector employment, people typically use their available resources such as time to deploy knowledge, assists, and suitability. The service industry involves service delivery to enterprises and consumers with an aim for profit. The services offered by the service sector may include shipment and transit of goods as well as the distribution and the sale of property from the manufacturer to the client or the consumer. This could happen whether in a retail shop or a wholesale store or merchandise.

On the other hand, creative industries involve the activities attached or correlated to the creation, manufacturing, and s=distribution of the original goods and services with integration of creative elements into the wider processes and other key sectors of the economy. Creative industries although they are not synonyms, they are also referring to as the cultural industries.

As or the United Nations Educational, Scientific and Cultural Organization, (UNESCO), the cultural industries are those that combine creation, manufacturing, and commercialization of the creative products that are not tangible and are cultural in type and display. Creative industries include the broader aspect of this through the inclusion both the cultural and artist works, be it a manufactured product or services.

As much as the service and creative industries seem not the same in their definition, the scope and objectives are visible from the definitions. The service industries concern much on the provision of services, and the creative industries involve too with services.

In our essay, we shall major on the service and creative industry, and shall define the service/creative industry as a sector of the economy that encompasses creation, production, disruption sale or marketing of any products as well as the provision of services which are creative ideas of individuals.

History

The service and creative industry have become the subject of scholar works and reviews in the early 19th century. However, the service sector and creative industry started long before the break of the world war one and two. During the world war, one people began to send spies to the countries which they thought was a threat to them. This substantially led to break out of allies and the start of the world one. During the world war, one service industry continued to manifest itself vividly. Soldiers dedicate to serve their country, and army helped and treated those soldiers who were shot by the enemies or by the injured during the war.

After the war, there was continued service by soldiers and secrets service men and women who went undercover to spy on the country enemies. The individuals used logs and mountain areas to drop their notes and information as well as to pick the information. This later advanced to be the mailing cooperation that used the pipes to send emails from one region to the other. Technology advancement led to the adoption of emails which were sent via mailing station and be transported via the trains and vehicles.

This is an example of how the service and creative industry has developed throughout its history. The service development history is also witnessed in education, health and communication sectors of the service sector.

AN ESSAY ON SERVICE AND CREATIVE INDUSTRY THEORY

Significance of a service/ creative industry

The service sector is one of the particular and most imperative industry since it interlinks all the area of the economy and is the greatest contributor to the economy. The primary area only produces the raw materials which are worthless to the clients, while the secondary sector industries and produces the products of the raw materials. But without the services sector, the goods produced can't reach the customers. The service sector is the intern link and serves bath the best interest and earns the profit for the both sides.

For instance in the medical service industries, even if the medicine manufacturing companies manufactures drugs and syringes. Who would be there to use them? It's in this case that the service and creative industry is a substantial and paramount sectored to consider. Roughly 95 percent of the world population mainly depend on the service and creative industry to acquire or to distribute their products.

The governments that have realized and invested in the service and creative industry have developed, and significant impact has realized in these countries. A good example for the case study in India. After India had realized that services sector is the backbone and can solve the problem of poverty, the government invested and directed their resources to health.

Today India is the hotbed and Hub for the best doctors and surgeons across the globe. Asians, Americans and some of the Africans are being sent to India for specializing medical care. This earns the governments alot of funds regarding taxe4s levied on the flights as well as taxes collected on the PR actioners pay. Research by the United Nations indicates that the poverty index of India has moved from 24 percent to 11 percent within a span of the last ten years. This shows the essence of boosting the creative and service industry of a country or bloc such as the European Union bloc or then African Union bloc.

Features of service/creative-industry

The service industry has distinctive characteristics that distinguish them from =any other industry or sector of the economy. Some of the distinguishing features include the following. As compare to any other area of the country's economy it is evident that the services offered are **intangible**. This because they are experiences created for the desired customers and consists of actions by the service provider as compared to the products provided by the manufacturer.

AN ESSAY ON SERVICE AND CREATIVE INDUSTRY THEORY

Services can be best described as the services which are intangibles since they are performances by people or company rather than actual objects, they can't be visible to the clients, can be felt, touched or tasted in as much as their counterparts in the industries which are products. In his works, Betason described this and termed intangibility as the substantial difference occurring between services and goods, from where the rest of the differences emerge.

This is one characteristic that is very different as compared to their industry. For instance, in the manufacturing sector a, the company may produce a new commodity and release it in the market. The company remains and owns the sole right of the produce and if anyone counterfeits the products the company may see the individual. On the other hand, the service and creative industry sector the services that are offered are intangible and hence can't be patented legally. This puts the services at a risk since they could be counterfeit easily by any other person who may benefit and the inventor of the services to never benefit.

Another distinctive characteristic that emerges in the creative industry is that there is **no accurate price** for the service puffer. By this, we compare the outcome of the service and that of the manufacturing sector. In the service sector, there is no an actual way to determine the actual cost of the unit of services, as well as the inconveniences, resulted from the quality of the service and the price to award to it. This makes it different from the manufacturing sector since the company keeps a record of the unit OD production and uses this to pin down the price of the product so as to gain profit. This differences service industry from the manufacturing sector.

The service/creative industries also have a distinctive characteristic of **inseparability**. By this, it means that products are created at some point by the manufacturers and are consumed by the clients in a simultaneous manner and can't be stored for a future use compared to goods. This implies that the customers or the consumers of a certain kind to be offered has to be present during the service production or the execution of the agreed service.

Hence services provided must be of high quality and those which are delivered within the desired time frame. This because in this service industry the clients influence other customers and their feedback after the service is the most paramount not even the service itself. (Lo lelock and gummesson 2004), summarized and said that the inseparability characterizes of service industry includes the presence of the clients, the client's roles as the main co-producer, customer to the employee and client to client interaction.

AN ESSAY ON SERVICE AND CREATIVE INDUSTRY THEORY

Compared to the primary sector of the economy which invites the raw materials, it is not a must to have a ready market for the raw materials to be extracted from the sources to companies for processing. Instead, the raw materials can just be obtained taken to the enterprise, and the products are manufactured and stored. Compared to the service industry where without bathing presence of the client or the consumers the service production is difficult if not entirely impossible.

The other distinctive characteristic is the **variability**. The service and creative industry face unique features since the services being rendered to the clients are not followed under a universal standard and guideline. Hence they face a challenge which is also a chastity's of achieving uniform output mostly for the labor-intensive service. This is not majorly on the service providers but also to the clients or consumers who have entirely different demands from each other.

For instance, two companies that manufacture the air conditioners have set guidelines and universal rules to follow in the production. This directive will result in a similar product if not a hundred percent. This makes it possible for the clients to choose from the products. The company products remain the same; the only modification can happen. Unlike in the service and creative industries where services are offered by individuals who are not restricted by hat standards and guidelines to meet.

This results in a scenario where an individual service provider produces a purely best service and another service provider in the same geographical location manage to give a relatively poor service. This clearly shows its distinctive characteristic compared to other sectors of the economy.

Consumer's demands also contribute to the variability of the service and creative industry since not all clients have universal needs. Some of the clients would prefer their service to be performed in a particular manner while the other individual may decline this. A good example of this is the car wash service industry, some of the car owners prefer they cash to be removed even in the inner parts. While others prefer them cars just to be wiped on the service. This difference in the consumer and clients' needs has been a topic for many.

Hence it would be more precise and profound to say that the essence and quality of the services provided occasionally vary from one producer to the other, client to client and from day to day with no factor held factor held constant.

Unlike the other two sectors of the economy, the products of the service industry are **perishable** and cannot be stored for future use or reuse. Therefore once an individual service has been rendered to the client at a certain point and time, it is quite had for the service to be sorted or reused again in life. For instance, if a producer is a medical professional and buffers a surgery service to the patient it is quite for the service to be stored or for it to be re-used again. Since the surgery neither can it be saved nor can it be re-administered unless recent surgery.

Unlike the manufacturing industry where the companies and the industries produce theater clothes and surgery gadgets. These products are stored till their urgency when they are recovered. They can also be reused primarily for the third garments, which are washed after the surgery and stored for reuse.

With this characterized the producers of the service industries are faced with one single challenge of ensuring that they offer their services and products within a short time frame. This becomes a problem to them.

Challenges facing Creative/service Industry

The creative and service industries have faced numerous challenges since it's unveiling till date. Some of these difficulties include the rapid change of environment. Using dynamics of the environment in the service and creative industry means that there has been changing and advancements in the technologies with a new digital migration shift, globalization, and the internet which has led to the loss of jobs or market for the services. For instance, in the early 20th century the mailing service industry was the best example one would use to research on the service sector. Today after the introduction of an email service by another service area producer the mailing Corporation have failed. This is one of the key challenge facing the creative service industry.'

The second challenge is the access to financial support from the banks and other lending institutions. The banking sector doesn't have the required expertise to be able to analyzed the business models in creative and service industries and did not value the products of their production. This economical and finical crisis makes the situation to be more critical and complicates the trade more. Since no service or creative industry can run or advance into the next level without financial and economic support. Hence the lack of access to or inadequate access to the finances from the banks is a subject to reevaluate critically.

AN ESSAY ON SERVICE AND CREATIVE INDUSTRY THEORY

Service and creative producers are individuals and most time they are cut in between the crossfire of national and the linguistic lines if politics is given a blind eye. According to research conducted by an independent survey, showed that consumers prefer to be served by individuals or creative producers who are of their same nationality or linguistic line. This jeopardizes the results since if the manufacturer realizes that most of the consumers prefer them to the others. They will give services that are of destitute quality/. Consequently, if the customer prefers to visit and get services from one producer leaving the rest, it is more likely that the rest will exit the business. If this challenged is not evaluated critically it may be the result of the failure in the creative and service industry in the 30th century.

Another challenge facing the creative services sector is the insufficient knowledge on the creative process and also the value of creativity to economy and culture. This is a challenge since most of the producers in the services industry do not give high-quality results as a result of poor quality. Henning is discouraging the consumers.

The other main challenge is the lack or an inadequate number of trained personnel in the rapid changing technology. This is a challenge since if the skills are not quickly modified to fit into the existing technology world, then it is more likely that the niche market need will not be kept arrive and may lead to the collapse of the industry.

Research shows that many of those individuals investing in the creative services sector are graduates from very highly recognized institutions who have high theoretical and creative skills but poor technical skills. This becomes a challenge since most of the work involved in the service and creative industries requires technical work such as washing the executive cars.

Another challenge facing the service sector id the failure to adopt business models that are common in the other two sectors of the economy. This leads to the incompetents and lack of strategic skills which are entirely necessary for the industry to have a high and quite sustained growth.

The other challenge is the lack of government recognition and support for the service and creative industry. This makes the industry to be viewed as the industry of the poor and the peasant citizens.

Conclusion

As examined in the research paper it is evident and clear that the service and the creative industry is a paramount and substantial sector in any economy. From the examples highlighted in the journal, it is more evident that were not for the dedication by the Indiana government to support and engage in the health serve industry the poverty index would not have declined instead it would have increased to 50 percent. The case studies encompassed in the research paper shows the significance of the industry to a country. The paper also offers recommendations to the challenges facing the industry.

References

Bilton, C., 2007. *Management and creativity: From creative industries to creative management*. Blackwell Publishing.

Daniels, P.W., 2014. 4 **SERVICE INDUSTRIES**: SOME NEW DIRECTIONS.*Progress in Industrial Geography (Routledge Revivals)*, p.111.

Dhar, R.L., 2015. **Service quality and the training of employees**: The mediating role of organizational commitment. *Tourism Management*, 46, pp.419-430.

Gibson, C. ed., 2014. *Creativity in peripheral places: Redefining the creative industries*. Routledge.

Hartley, J. ed., 2005. *Creative industries* (pp. xvii-414). Blackwell Pub..

Hartley, J., 2014. **Renewing Place, Knowledge, Economy, Culture**–The creative industries agenda for the global, digital era. In *A Study of Creative Industries:"The Queensland Model"* (pp. 1-21). Economic Science Press.

Hracs, B.J. and Leslie, D., 2014. **Aesthetic labour in creative industries**: the case of independent musicians in Toronto, Canada. *Area*, 46(1), pp.66-73.

Sharma, V. and Sonwalkar, J., 2016. **Consumer retention strategies for telecom service industry in India**: a theoretical perspective. *Journal of Management Research and Analysis*, 3(3), pp.110-121.

Yang, C.C., Cheng, L.Y. and Lin, C.J., 2015. **A typology of customer variability and employee variability in service industries**. *Total Quality Management & Business Excellence*, 26(7-8), pp.825-839.

YOUR KNOWLEDGE HAS VALUE

- We will publish your bachelor's and
  master's thesis, essays and papers

- Your own eBook and book -
  sold worldwide in all relevant shops

- Earn money with each sale

Upload your text at www.GRIN.com
and publish for free